You're

Sheila H
and Isab
illustrate

Books Beyond Words

Gaskell Press/St. George's Hospital Medical School
LONDON

First published in Great Britain 1996 by St. George's Hospital Medical School and Gaskell Press

ISBN 1 901242 00 5

British Library Cataloguing-in-Publication Data.
A catalogue record for this book is available from the British Library.

Printed and bound in Great Britain by Acanthus Press Limited, Wellington, Somerset TA21 8ST

Further information about the Books Beyond Words series can be obtained from:
Royal College of Psychiatrists
17, Belgrave Square
London SW1X 8PG
Tel. 0171 235 2351
Fax: 0171 245 1231

Dedicated to people with learning disabilities or mental health needs who have experienced the criminal justice system at first hand, often without good guidance.

Acknowledgements

Many people gave their time most generously, in particular: Kay Beaumont, Shelley Burke, David Carson, Elaine Crick, Dorothea Duncan, Nigel Hollins, Raymond Holyhead, Pat Howlin, Rod Jarman, Monica Kelly, Freda Macey, Nicholas Markendale, Sally Miller, Zenobia Nadirshaw, Karen Page, Clive Pearman, David Redston, Michael Speed, Margaret Stark, Chris Williams, Tom Williamson. Thanks are also due to Avon and Somerset Police (Taunton), Petty Sessional Divisions of Taunton Deane and West Somerset (Taunton), and the Press Office, H.M. Prison Services.

We are grateful to Mencap for financial support to this project.

Please note

The order of the pictures and text is intended to follow the procedures used by police and magistrates in England and Wales. However, it cannot be used as a precise guide to procedure for three reasons: first, the exact procedure varies slightly even within England and Wales, according to local working practices; second, the exact events in any one case will vary with the requirements of the case; lastly, this is a story intended to show the likely events, but unable to show all possible events when someone with learning disabilities or mental health needs comes into contact with the criminal justice system.

COURT

13

15

18

19

COURT

29

Dave's story

This book is about what happens when someone is **accused*** of a crime. It will help you if you have been accused of a crime and have to go to court for a trial.

Lots of people's stories will fit this book. The pictures suit any crime. We have told one story below. In our story we see what happens to Dave when he has to go on trial in a Magistrates' court. You can see what a Magistrates' Court looks like in this book.

Some people have to go to a Crown Court instead of a Magistrates' Court. This is usually because they have been accused of a more serious crime. Magistrates Courts and Crown courts are different. Crown Courts have a judge and jury and the lawyers have to wear wigs and gowns. Magistrates Courts usually have three Magistrates and people dress in ordinary clothes. (You can see what Crown Courts look like in the book about being a witness in court, called *'Going to Court'*).

If the police think you have done a crime, they will question you before you go to court. You may want to read about what happens at the police station in the book *'You're under Arrest'*. Then you can read this one later.

Please note – words which are written **like this** with * next to them are explained in the **Notes** at the end.

Picture numbers:

1. Dave is in the street. The police tell him to get in the police car. They tell him "You're under arrest."
2. Dave is taken to the police station. The police woman is asking Dave about what happened.

She is recording what they say on tape. Dave has a **solicitor*** and someone called Richard to help him. Richard is the **"Appropriate Adult"***.

3. Dave is being charged by the police. This means he may have to go to court.

4. Dave is having his fingerprints taken.

5. Dave is having his photograph taken.

6. The **Custody Officer*** took Dave's things to keep them safe when he arrived at the Police Station. Now he is giving them back.

7. Dave is allowed to go home. This is called being given **bail***. He is very tired. He knows he will have to go to court another day.

8. Dave is at home. Richard is helping him mark the calendar so he knows what day to go to court.

9. Dave is talking to his solicitor. She helps him fill in a form for **legal aid***. He tells his solicitor why he is under arrest. She explains what will happen in court. She helps him decide if he will **plead* guilty*** or **not guilty*** in court.

10. Today Dave is going to the Magistrates' Court. Richard goes with him. Dave is feeling nervous. He is not sure what it will be like.

11. The man at the desk inside the court building is called the **usher***. He asks Dave's name. He tells Dave and Richard which courtroom to go to. The building is big and confusing.

12. Dave and Richard meet with the solicitor again and then they wait for their turn in the court. Dave has to wait a long time. It is busy and noisy. Dave gets very nervous. He is glad Richard is with him.

13. The court usher tells Dave to come into the court. He shows him where to sit. Dave will probably have to sit on his own but Richard might be allowed to sit with him. Dave can see the three **Magistrates*** behind the desk at the front. He feels scared.

14. There are a lot of people in court. He can see his solicitor and Richard. He is not allowed to talk to Richard. He could talk to his solicitor if he needs to.

15. The Clerk of the Court sits just in front of the Magistrates. She asks Dave to say his name and where he lives. She reads out the charge and asks Dave if he is pleading guilty or not guilty. Dave pleads not guilty. The trial will be on another day. The Magistrates say Dave can go home on bail. Sometimes the Magistrates do not allow people to go home to wait for the trial. They may have to go to prison or hospital to wait (**Remand in custody***).

    (Some people plead guilty. Then there is no trial and no witnesses are called. The Magistrates can ask for **a pre-sentence report*** or they can give **a sentence*** straight away.)

16. Dave is back home. He and Richard are reading this book. Dave is trying to understand what will happen next time he goes to court.

17. Dave is very fed up. He feels it will never end.

18. Dave goes to court for the trial. There are lots of people again. There are three Magistrates again. Often the Magistrates are different each time people go back to court.

19. A woman goes into the witness box. She promises to tell the truth. The **prosecution solicitor*** from the **CPS*** asks her questions. She says she saw Dave doing a crime. Then Dave's solicitor asks her questions.

    Sometimes there are lots of witnesses. They each have to go in the witness box for questions.

20. Now it is Dave's turn. He **takes the oath***. This means he promises to tell the truth about exactly what happened.

21. Dave's solicitor asks him questions. Dave knows her. She helps Dave tell the court what happened.

22. Then the prosecution solicitor asks him questions. Dave does not know this solicitor. He says Dave did the crime. Dave feels upset.

    Dave's solicitor can ask some more questions after the prosecution solicitor has finished.

23. The Magistrates listen to the witnesses and the solicitors and to Dave. They decide whether they think Dave is guilty or not guilty.

    If they think he is not guilty he can just go home and that will be the end of the court case.

    If they think he is guilty they will **sentence*** him. The Magistrates may ask for a **Pre-Sentence Report*** from a **Probation Officer*** before they sentence Dave, to help them decide on what sentence is best.

    In this story, the Magistrates think Dave is guilty and they ask the Probation Officer for a Pre-Sentence Report. The Magistrates tell Dave to come back to court in a few weeks time after he has talked to the Probation Officer.

24. Then the Magistrates leave the court. Dave can go home if he has bail.

25. Dave is meeting with the Probation Officer. He is asking Dave about his life. He asks Dave about his difficulties and whether he has been to court before. He also asks Dave a lot about why he is under arrest.

    The Probation Officer may also visit Dave at home and speak to people there who know him.

26. The Probation Officer writes a report about Dave for the court.

27. The Probation Officer explains his report to Dave.

28. Dave goes back to court.

29. In court, the Probation Officer gives the report to the Magistrates and to Dave's solicitor. Richard can see the report too if Dave says that is okay. The prosecution solicitor does not get a copy of the report.

30. Dave is waiting in court while the Magistrates decide what to do. Dave is fed up. He is worried about what will happen to him.

31. Everyone stands up when the Magistrates come in. Dave is scared. He knows they might send him to prison.

32. The Magistrates say what they have decided. They say what will happen to Dave, what his sentence is.

33. This picture shows some of the things which might happen to Dave. There are lots of different kinds of sentence.

- The Magistrates could **fine*** him or give him **a conditional discharge*** which means he can go home (top left picture with a yellow border).

- They could put him **on Probation*.** This means he can still live at home. He will have to see a Probation Officer quite often and he may have to see a **Mental Health Worker*** who could be a clinical psychologist, a psychiatrist, a community nurse or a social worker for help or treatment (bottom left picture with a green border).

- They could send him to hospital (top right picture with a blue border).

- Or the Magistrates could send him to prison (bottom right picture with a red border).

Whatever happens, Dave now has a **criminal record*.**

Notes

Accused: When the Prosecution tells the court you did a crime, they are accusing *you* of doing it.

Defence Solicitor (or Barrister):

A solicitor (or barrister) is someone who is trained in the Law. The **Defence** solicitor is the lawyer who will help you in court to say what you think happened. If you have no money, you can get "**Legal Aid**" (money from the government) to pay him or her. The Defence solicitor will help you fill in the form to apply for Legal Aid.

Appropriate Adult:

If you have learning disabilities or mental health problems the police have to call someone to help you at the police station. They should also call someone if you went to a special school or cannot read. The person is called the Appropriate Adult. The person might be from your family or someone you know. The police have a list of Appropriate Adults they can call in.

Custody Officer:

The Custody Officer is a police officer. His or her job is to look after all the people who are under arrest. Tell the Custody Officer if you have any special needs, like for tablets or for special help. Tell the Custody Officer if you feel ill or upset.

Bail: This is when the police or a court decides you can go home to wait for the next time you come to court. Sometimes the bail conditions say where you must live or that you must not go to a particular place. Sometimes there may be other conditions

Plead: If you tell the court you did do the crime, you plead **guilty**. That means you say you did do it. If you tell the court you did not do the crime, you plead **not guilty.** That means you say you did not do it.

Usher:

The usher shows people where to go in the Magistrates' Court.

Magistrates:

The Magistrates are in charge of what happens in court. Their job is to listen to what everyone says and decide if the person did the crime. They also decide the sentence.

Remand (in custody): This is when the court decides you have to go to prison or to hospital to wait for the trial. Sometimes the court asks the hospital to write a report about you. The report goes to the court next time you go.

Pre-Sentence Report (or PSR): This is the name for the report the Probation Officer writes, to help the court decide what to do.

**Prosecution Solicitor
(or Barrister):**

This is the lawyer who will say in court that you did do a crime. He (or she) does not talk to you outside the court about what really happened. In court he sometimes seems to be horrible to you, but he is just doing a job.

Crown Prosecution Service (or CPS): This is the name for the lawyers who look at the facts the police collect about your case. They decide if you should go to court or not. Lots of lawyers work for the Crown Prosecution Service.

Oath: In court you have to promise to tell the truth about what happened. You can put your hand on the Bible to promise or on another religious book like the Koran. Tell the court usher what religion you believe in so s/he can give you the right book. If you are not religious, you can just promise. This is called **affirming**.

Probation Officer:

This is a person who works for the Probation service. Probation Officers write reports for the court. Their reports help the Magistrates decide on a sentence for someone who has done a crime. They also help people who have done a crime to stop doing any more crimes. They are told who to help by the court.

Sentence: This is what the Magistrates say will happen to you if they think you did the crime. There are lots of different sentences. The sentence might be any of the things in this list.

- to go to **prison**.
- to go to a **psychiatric hospital or a hospital for people with learning disabilities or a Special Hospital** under the Mental Health Act. This means you won't be able to leave the hospital until the doctors and social workers think you are ready.
- to go on a **guardianship order under the Mental Health Act**. This means that you have a guardian. The guardian is often a social worker. He or she can tell you
  - where to live.
  - or to go to a day centre.
  - or to go for treatment.
  - or to do all of these things.
- to go on a **probation order,** which will mean seeing the Probation Officer lots of times. Sometimes the court adds conditions to the probation order.
  - the court can tell you where to live.
  - or to go to a day centre.
  - or to go for treatment.
- to do some **community service**. This means working in the community at some kind of job. The Magistrates will say how many hours you must do. The Probation Officer will talk to you about what you will do. The Probation Officer will check you do it. You do not get paid for this job.

- some sentences mean you must not commit another crime. For example, **a conditional discharge or a suspended sentence or being bound over**. These sentences mean that you can go free but you must not do another crime. If you do another crime, or get into trouble you may have to go back to court.

- to pay a **fine**. This means you have to pay some money. The Magistrates will say how much you have to pay.

- an **absolute discharge**. This means you can just go home. You do not have to do anything special.

Mental Health Worker:

This is someone like a community nurse or psychiatrist or clinical psychologist or social worker who works with you and with people who care for you, like your family or support workers at your house. The mental health worker will give you support and treatment so you are less likely to go on trial again.

Criminal Record: If you have been found guilty of a crime in court, your name, address, the crime and the sentence are written down. The police will put this information on the police computer. This list of people and their crimes can be looked at by the police whenever they like. They can also keep your photo and fingerprints which they took at the police station.

If you are found not guilty in court, your name does not go on this list. Then you have no criminal record and the police have to throw away your photo and fingerprints.